Royal Bota

Bible plants at Kew

F Nigel Hepper

London: Her Majesty's Stationery Office

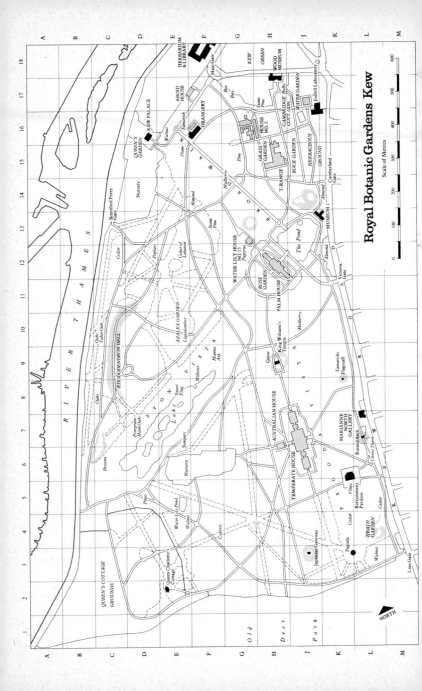

Royal Botanic Gardens Kew

NORTH

Scale of Metres

0   100   200   300   400   500   600

Contents

Introduction

ost of the plants mentioned in the Bible come from the eastern Mediterranean region, present-day Israel, Jordan, Lebanon and Syria, often termed the Holy Land. However, we also read of Arabian spices, Egyptian vegetables, African woods and Indian perfumes. Such a wide distribution involves a range of climate from the snows of Mount Lebanon to the tropical heat of Africa. Yet at the Royal Botanic Gardens, Kew, many of these plants may be seen growing out of doors or in the greenhouses. The Kew Museums also display examples of timbers and other useful plant products mentioned in the Bible. This booklet provides the visitor to Kew with a guide to their whereabouts as they are not grouped together in a special biblical garden. The indexes (pages 54–64) show not only the page references but the locations at Kew.

The study of ancient and biblical plants is nothing new at Kew since a former Director, Sir Joseph Hooker (1817–1911), and a Curator of the Gardens, John Smith the elder (1797–1888), were both knowledgeable on the subject. In 1860 Hooker visited the Holy Land, then under the control of Turkey and difficult of access compared with modern package tours! Erudite articles on the plants were written by him and published in William Smith's *Dictionary of the Bible* (1863). John Smith never had the opportunity to travel to the Holy Land, but he studied Hooker's material and gathered information from many sources for his book *History of Bible Plants* (1878). As he was blind at the time he dictated the text to a woman secretary.

Since Smith's day huge strides have been made in the study of the plants of the Holy Land. Much research has been carried out by resident botanists in the region and I have had the privilege of travelling with some of them in order to see the living plants in the field. Thus I have been able to visit Egypt, Yemen, Israel, Jordan, Turkey, Greece and Italy, besides tropical Africa and Sri Lanka.

Many problems remain, however, and this booklet is not the place to discuss them. But one can sympathize with the linguistic scholars who were unable to recognize the plants and animals mentioned in the Old Testament written in Hebrew and the New Testament written in Greek. Frequently the line of least resistance was taken and the name inserted of an organism likely to be known to the readers. Other translators were more scientific in their approach, although sometimes even now it is difficult to know what species was intended because the original authors were not naturalists and they used imprecise terms.

There are other considerations for the modern Bible reader. Ours is an age of sophisticated city-dwellers, who often find it difficult to appreciate how close to the land the people lived in biblical times. Most of them were peasant farmers, and even townsmen had farms or orchard-gardens beyond the city walls. Fuel was gathered from the wooded hillsides and most people were knowledgeable about the use of wild plants for food and medicine.

Notes on the arrangement

The following brief account is arranged partly by location of the exhibits at Kew and partly according to the habit or properties of the plants concerned. However, it is impossible to reconcile conflicting choices of placement to be entirely logical, and the reader is referred to the indexes and map in order to trace the description and whereabouts of any species. Short background descriptions are added, together with some references to the scriptural context in which the species is mentioned.

References to the chapters and verses in the Bible are cited and, because there is considerable variation in translations, the version may be indicated. The following abbreviations are used:

AV King James's Authorized Version (1611)
RSV Revised Standard Version (Nelson 1952)
NEB New English Bible (Oxford 1961 and 1970)
TEV Today's English Version, the Good News Bible (The Bible Societies 1976)
NIV New International Version (Hodder & Stoughton 1979)

For a fuller treatment readers are referred to *The Illustrated Bible Dictionary* and other works in the list on page 51.

Bible gardens

It is likely that this guide will have a wider application than Kew since many of the plants can be seen in public and private gardens, as well as in museums, in Europe and elsewhere. It should also be helpful for gardening enthusiasts who wish to group together some of these species into biblical gardens. Several Bible gardens are actually in existence, such as the one beside the cathedral at Bangor, North Wales. In Australia there is another at Palm Beach, Sydney. In the USA the Missouri Botanical Garden has a collection in the Mediterranean house and the New York Botanical Garden has staged special exhibitions on the subject. There are also gardens run by some American churches, such as the one at the Cathedral Church of St John the Divine, New York; and a new one at Grove Avenue Baptist Church, Richmond, Virginia, which I recently designed. The Amsterdam Free University celebrated its centenary in 1980 with a comprehensive exhibition of bible plants. In Israel there is the recent development of Neot Kedumim, 'The Gardens of Israel'. This 400-acre estate on the hillsides between Tel-Aviv and Jerusalem is directed by Nogah Hareuveni and displays biblical plants and others associated with Hebrew traditions.

Bible gardens established in places where the climate is

different from that obtaining in the Near East may find the establishment of biblical species difficult or impossible. One way is to plant species of the same genus (or of similar appearance) that are known to be tolerant of the conditions under which they will be grown. In the same way in this booklet I have referred to related plants when the actual species is not represented at Kew.

Another difficulty occurs for those wishing to establish a full collection of biblical plants. This concerns the availability of the seeds or cuttings. While many of them are common and easily obtained from commercial sources, some are rarely cultivated and difficult to obtain. It is regretted, however, that for obvious reasons Kew cannot undertake to supply requests for such plants. Nevertheless, an interesting and representative collection can readily be built up as a beautiful and instructive Bible garden following careful thought and planning.

A word of caution to visitors

Visitors to Kew should not expect to see all of these plants at one time of the year, and certainly not in one day. Besides their being widely scattered throughout the 300-acre grounds of Kew, many plants are seasonal in appearance. Thus annuals need to be sown each year and they are visible only during their growing season. Perennial plants usually die down after flowering and they may remain dormant for several months. Although trees and shrubs can be seen throughout the year, there is a period when they are at their best.

Moreover, there are often changes in the plantings at Kew. Species may be discontinued or to be seen in different places than indicated at the time of writing (1981). Similarly the Museum displays are subject to changes. On the other hand it is possible that in time there will be additional displays in both the Gardens and the Museums to those indicated. Most of the greenhouses open daily throughout the year, except when closed for maintenance. House No.15, however, is closed during the winter months.

1 Cedar of Lebanon and other trees
Forest trees at Kew and their timbers

I the LORD . . . will put in the wilderness the cedar and the acacia, the myrtle and the olive. I will set in the desert the cypress, the plane and the pine together.
(Isaiah 41:19 RSV)

an has always been fascinated by trees and they often have religious significance. They certainly take a prominent place in the Bible from Genesis (2:9) where we meet with the tree of life and the tree of the knowledge of good and evil, to Revelation (22:2,14) where the tree of life is mentioned again. Between these first and final books there are many descriptions of trees and allusions to them. Their great size and durability, their beauty and desirability, and their greenness contrasting with thorniness, all find a place. Jotham's story of the anointing of the king of the trees features in the Old Testament (Judges 9:7–15), while in the New Testament Jesus taught a lesson from the fig tree (Matthew 24:32).

Many of the forest trees mentioned in the Bible grow well at Kew. They are scattered throughout the Gardens and several flat-topped old cedars of Lebanon *(Cedrus libani)* remind us of the timber used for the building of King Solomon's house and temple about 950 BC (1 Kings 5). Thousands of men laboured high up on Mt Lebanon felling the giant trees and transporting them to the coast, where they were floated southwards to near the present Tel-Aviv before being hauled all the way up to Jerusalem. Other coniferous trees were used, such as Aleppo pines *(Pinus halepensis)*, juniper *(Juniperus drupacea, J. excelsa)* and cypress *(Cupressus sempervirens)*. These and similar species occur at Kew in the pinetum lying south of the Lake. Samples of some of their timbers can be seen on display in the Wood Museum and in the Marianne North Gallery.

A stately cedar of Lebanon *(Cedrus libani)* in front of the Pagoda at Kew (p. 8)

An Aleppo pine *(Pinus halepensis)* in the Arboretum (p. 8)

The oleander *(Nerium oleander)* is also called the rose of Jericho (p. 16)

Poppy anemones *(Anemone coronaria)*, often considered to be the 'lily of the field', seen in Cambridge Cottage Garden (p. 20)

◁ This oriental plane tree *(Platanus orientalis)*, seen in winter mist, was planted at Kew in 1762 (pp. 15, 16)

Flax plants *(Linum usitatissimum)* flowering in the Herbaceous Ground at Kew (p. 20)

Dill *(Anethum graveolens)* was one of the spices tithed by Scribes and Pharisees (p. 25)

In the wooded area between the Rhododendron Dell and the River Thames one can see oak trees from the Mediterranean region. The Tabor oak *(Quercus ithaburensis)* is deciduous and a young tree raised in 1967 from Israeli seed is numbered 1058 on its label. It is similar to the Valonia oak *(Q. aegilops)*, also growing in the collection. The eastern Mediterranean form of the evergreen Kermes oak *(Quercus coccifera* or *Q. calliprinos)* is often shrubby, though it can look similar to the holm oak *(Q. ilex)*, which is common at Kew, but native to the central and western Mediterranean region. It is interesting to note that scale insects infesting Kermes oaks provided the scarlet dye used for the Tabernacle (Exodus 36:35) and the Temple curtain (2 Chronicles 3:14). Oaks and other trees were traditionally planted or preserved near graves, while the hard timber was suitable for carving heathen idols (Isaiah 44:14) and ships' oars (Ezekiel 27:6). A portion of 'Abraham's oak' at Hebron, as well as cedar wood from Lebanon, was brought back by Sir Joseph Hooker for the Kew Museums reference collection.

It is not always clear from the biblical Hebrew whether an oak or a kind of terebinth *(Pistacia atlantica)* was intended, as their names are similar (in fact, the leafless trees have a similar appearance). Thus, the tree in which Absalom was hung up by

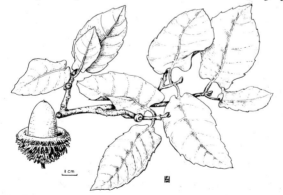

Mount Tabor oak *(Quercus ithaburensis)*, one of the oak trees of Israel

his hair (2 Samuel 18:9) could have been of either kind. *P. atlantica* is too tender to be grown outside at Kew but a small example may be seen in the south block of the Temperate House where the terebinths *P. terebinthus* and *P. palaestina*, are also grown. A third *Pistacia* species is present there, too, which is the lentisk *(P. lentiscus)* that commonly occurs in thickets on Mediterranean hillsides. It yields the resin known as mastic, a sample of which is on display in Museum No. 1. This resin was used in ancient Egyptian embalming and is nowadays used as a varnish. It may have been the balm taken to Egypt by Joseph's captors (Genesis 37:25), though other suggestions are made on p. 38. Also in the Temperate House is the N. African coniferous tree *Tetraclinis articulata*. Roman cabinet-makers favoured the thyine wood from this tree (Revelation 18:12). It also produces sandarac resin used for varnish and incense.

Other trees of the Mediterranean hillsides include the box-tree *(Buxus sempervirens)* (Isaiah 41:19 and 60:13 AV, Ezekiel 27:6 NEB) and the bay-tree or true laurel *(Laurus nobilis)* (Psalm 37:35 AV) from which emperors' and athletes' leafy crowns were made (1 Corinthians 9:25). Cultivars of the box-tree edge the beds in the Queen's Garden, where in summertime there are potted bay-trees. Full-grown small trees of both species can be seen in the shrubberies near the Main Gate. A very different crown may have been made from the small tree known as Christ's thorn *(Paliurus spina-christi)*. As its name implies, it is one of the plants thought to have been used for the crown of thorns placed on Jesus' head at his crucifixion (Matthew 27:29; John 19:2). As can be seen on the bush of it near the Ruined Arch, it has a pair of very sharp stipular thorns at the base of each leaf, one being straight and the other reflexed. Two other plants that some writers consider could have been used for the crown of thorns are *Ziziphus spina-christi* (in the Temperate House) and the spiny burnet, *Poterium spinosum* (which is sometimes grown in sheltered spots in the Rock Garden).

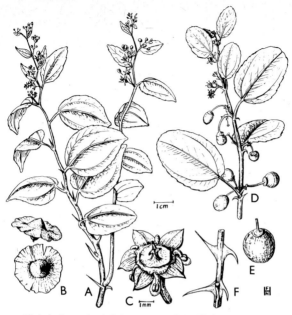

The two Christ's thorns (a–c) *Paliurus spina-christi* (d–f) *Ziziphus spina-christi*

Poplars *(Populus euphratica)*, willows *(Salix acmophylla, S. subserrata)* and plane-trees *(Platanus orientalis)* often grow beside Near Eastern streams and rivers (Psalm 1:3, Jeremiah 17:8). Jacob peeled off the bark of white poplar *(Populus alba)* and plane, as well as almond, so that the streaked twigs would increase the number of pied animals in his herds (Genesis 30:37–43). The rustling of poplar leaves was the sign for David's men to attack the Philistines (2 Samuel 5:23,24). The 'willows' on which the exiled Israelites hung their musical instruments grew beside the rivers of Babylon (Psalm 137:2). These were the Euphrates popular and not the weeping willow *(Salix babylonica)*, in spite of its epithet, since it is usually considered to have originated in China. Weeping willows and other species similar to the Near Eastern willows and poplars grow by the

Lake and the Pond opposite the Palm House. A large tree of the eastern plane *(Platanus orientalis)* stands by the western end of the Orangery.

Some authors consider that the biblical willows were the oleander bush *(Nerium oleander)*, which is indeed frequent in seasonal stream beds in the Holy Land. However, it seems that oleander is referred to only in the Apocrypha, where it is mentioned as the 'rose plant in Jericho' or 'the rose growing by the brook' (Ecclesiasticus 24:12 and 39:13). Tubs of oleanders are usually placed in the courtyard of the Queen's Garden, where they flower beautifully in midsummer. Others flower for much of the year in the Temperate House.

Elijah sat down to rest under a broom tree when fleeing from Jezebel (1 Kings 19:4 AV juniper). The white broom of the desert *(Retama raetam)* is similar to broom bushes with white flowers at Kew, although in a different genus *(Cytisus)*. They flower in April and May on Mount Pleasant near the Lake.

Tamarisk trees prefer saline soil and seasonal stream beds in the Near East. Abraham planted one in the desert at Beersheba (Genesis 21:33). At Kew several of these feathery bushes *(Tamarix gallica*, *T. parviflora)* can be seen near the flagstaff and others behind the Orangery. Because aphids feeding on tamarisks exude a sweet resin, it has been suggested that this was the manna that sustained the Israelites in the wilderness (Exodus 16:4, 14–35 etc.). Indeed, there is even one called *Tamarix gallica* var. *mannifera* – i.e. the manna bearer. Other authors consider the manna was a lichen *(Lecanora)*, although this desert plant has not been recorded from Sinai, or a purely miraculous provision, like the burning bush (Exodus 3:2–4). There is also the so-called manna ash *(Fraxinus ornus)* from Syria, trees of which stand near the east end of the Lake and are spectacular in May, but this could not have been the manna of the Israelites. (The book by Donkin (1980) indicated in Further Reading gives an account of these and other sources of manna.)

2 Lilies of the field
Plants in the Herbaceous Ground

Why are you anxious about clothing? Consider the lilies of the field. (Matthew 6:28 RSV)

lthough some of the herbaceous plants mentioned in the Bible are grown in various parts of Kew, others are grouped in the Herbaceous Ground, which was formerly known as the Order Beds, in which the plant families are arranged according to the Bentham and Hooker system. In the following account, the plant families are listed alphabetically. Many of the bulbous monocotyledons are grown in the Bulb Garden (H17), which is part of Cambridge Cottage Garden, and cereals in the Grass Garden (H15).

Chenopodiaceae The spinach and beetroot family. A plant with salty leaves or an inhabitant of saline soil is implied in Job 30:4 (AV, RSV mallow; NEB saltwort; TEV plants of the desert; NIV salt herbs). This is salt-bush *(Atriplex halimus)* ; several species of *Atriplex* are grown in this bed.

Compositae These beds contain the daisy family, many members of which flower in late summer. Several of the thistles that occur in the Holy Land are grown in them. The milk thistle *(Silybum marianum)* and the Syrian thistle *(Notobasis syriaca)* have beautifully mottled, prickly leaves and pink flowers on tall stems throughout the summer. They grow in masses at the edges of cornfields suffocating the young grain, so they probably were the 'thorns' referred to in the parable of the sower in Matthew 13:7,22.

Thistles and thorns are often mentioned in the Bible and their precise identification is uncertain (Genesis 3:18; 2 Kings 14:9; Job 31:40; Hosea 10:8; Matthew 7:16). For example, the spotted golden thistle *(Scolymus maculatus)* and the star thistle *(Centaurea calcitrapa)*, both usually grown in the Herbaceous Ground, are frequent weeds in the Holy Land.

To the same family belong the yellow crown daisy *(Chrysanthemum coronarium)* and species of the white-rayed chamomile *(Anthemis)*. It has been suggested, that these, rather than the poppy anemone, were the flowers of the field that Jesus compared with the glory of Solomon (Matthew 6:28 AV, RSV lilies).

The genus *Artemisia* has several species similar in appearance to one another with grey-green leaves. The desert *A. herba-alba* and *A. judaica* yield bitter juice which is referred to in the Bible as wormwood (Deuteronomy 29:18; Revelation 8:10–11).

The bitter herbs eaten by Jews at Passover (Exodus 12:8; Numbers 9:11) include endive and chicory *(Cichorium endivia, C. intybus)*, lettuce *(Lactuca sativa)* and dandelion *(Taraxacum officinale)*, all in this family, although they are not necessarily the ones used in biblical times.

Cruciferae The cabbage or wallflower family. The mustard seed of the Bible (Matthew 13:31, 17:20) is usually said to be the plant we know as black mustard *(Brassica nigra)*. It is an annual with bright yellow flowers. Others have suggested the similar white mustard *(Sinapis alba)*. Mustard seeds are displayed in Museum No.1.

Euphorbiaceae The spurge family. Towards the Jodrell Laboratory these beds contain several large castor-oil plants *(Ricinus communis)*. This is popularly considered to be the plant that grew rapidly and sheltered Jonah while he waited to see what would become of the wicked city of Nineveh (Jonah 4:6). However, the AV translation of the Hebrew word *qiqayon* is 'gourd' and one can certainly imagine a cucumber-like plant climbing over Jonah's booth, rather than a castor-oil bush.

Labiatae   This is the mint family of which many species, such as *Mentha longifolia*, were used for flavouring in New Testament times (Matthew 23:23; Luke 11:42).

Another member of the mint family is the Judean sage *(Salvia judaica)* which some authors considered inspired the design of the seven-branched lampstand (or 'candlestick'), the Menorah of the Hebrews (Exodus 37:17–18). Similar species of sage *(Salvia)* are grown in this bed.

Leguminosae   The pea and bean family. Lentils *(Lens culinaris)* were a favourite vegetable from very early times in the Old Testament. Jacob tricked Esau by offering red lentil stew (Genesis 25:29–34). Lentils, like many other vetches and pulses, are rich in protein. Some ancient samples are on display in Museum No. 1. Broadbeans *(Vicia faba)* and chickpeas *(Cicer arietinum)* may have been the 'pulses' Daniel and his friends ate instead of the King's rich food (Daniel 1:12).

Liliaceae   The lily family. At the foot of the western boundary wall of the Herbaceous Ground are various onions *(Allium* species). These recall the yearnings by the Israelites for their favourite onions *(A. cepa)*, leeks *(A. porrum* or *A. kurrat)* and garlic *(A. sativum)* during their wandering in the Sinai Desert (Numbers 11:5).

Nearby are several species of the Star-of-Bethlehem *(Ornithogalum)* known in the Bible as 'dove's dung' owing to their abundance on Mediterranean hillsides where the white flowers appear like bird droppings. It was probably the small bulbs of *O. narbonense* that were eaten in times of famine (2 Kings 6:25), since other species are known to be poisonous.

The 'lilies' mentioned in Song of Solomon (2:1, 4:5, 6:2 etc.) have been the source of much discussion. They could be the hyacinth *(Hyacinthus orientalis)* or the Madonna lily *(Lilium candidum*, see note on p. 39) or other showy species. Because the Hebrew word for lily is *shushan* it has been suggested that the

Iranian city of Susa or Shushan (Nehemiah 1:1, Esther 1:2) was named after the stately crown imperial *(Fritillaria imperialis)* which occurs in the region. It flowers in March. Many of these bulbs are grown in the Cambridge Cottage Garden.

Linaceae   In this bed grows a clump of the flax plant *(Linum usitatissimum)*. Fine-quality linen cloth is still made from the stems of this blue-flowered annual, which is one of the world's most ancient textile plants. Jewish priests in Old Testament times had to wear linen while officiating at sacrifices (Leviticus 6:10), and much later Jesus' body was wrapped in a linen shroud (Matthew 27:59; John 19:40). The glossy seeds of flax yield the well-known linseed oil. Ancient Egyptian linen is shown in Museum No. 1.

Papaveraceae   The glorious scarlet poppies *(Papaver* species*)* could also have been referred to as biblical lilies (see cover).

Ranunculaceae   Buttercup family. The black cumin *(Nigella sativa)* with greenish-blue flowers are less decorative than the closely related love-in-a-mist of gardens. Black cumin (called 'fitches' in the Authorised Version) were mentioned by Isaiah (28:25 and 27) as one of the plants that must be threshed gently with sticks to avoid damaging the spicy seeds.

The poppy anemone *(Anemone coronaria)* is popularly considered to be the wild flower or lily of the field of Matthew 6:28 (but see *Papaveraceae* and *Compositae* for other suggestions). It is one of the most splendid flowers of early spring in the Holy Land, still growing among the rocks around Jerusalem. (Plants can be seen in the bulb beds in Cambridge Cottage Garden, if not in the Herbaceous Ground).

Rosaceae   For 'rose' see p. 42.

Rutaceae   For rue *(Ruta graveolens, R. chalepensis)* see p. 40.

ABOVE: a flower-head of milk thistle *(Silybum marianum)* and detail of its beautifully mottled leaf (pp. 17, 39). BELOW: the spotted golden thistle *(Scolymus maculatus)* is another prickly plant (p. 18)

Vitis vinifera

A grape vine in flower *(Vitis vinifera)* ; a painting by Ferdinand Bauer in
Sibthorp's *Flora Graeca* (1819) (p. 27)

◁ TOP: crown daisy *(Chrysanthemum coronarium)*, a common wild flower in the
Holy Land (p. 18). LEFT: flowers of chicory *(Cichorium intybus)*, one of the
bitter herbs eaten at Passover (p. 18). RIGHT: the white flowers of this
star-of-Bethlehem *(Ornithogalum narbonense)*, look like 'dove's dung' (p. 19)

Apricot *(Prunus armenaica)* fruiting against a wall in Switzerland (p. 31)

Almond tree *(Prunus dulcis)* in full flower at Kew in early spring (p. 31)

Solanaceae The potato and nightshade family. The dark-green leafy rosettes of the mandrake *(Mandragora officinarum)* may be seen during the first half of the year. The mandrake has a long history of magic and superstition, especially as a fertility cult. This explains the argument between Leah and the childless Rachel related in Genesis 30:14. It flowers very early in the year and the fruits are like small yellow eggs on the ground, sometimes ripening at Kew. They are fragrant when ripe and this curious scent was referred to by Solomon in an amorous context (Song of Solomon 7:13). Its taproot forks and can be imagined to look like a person – it was said to shriek on pulling up, so a dog was made to do the job!

The brier of Micah 7:4 is said to be *Solanum incanum*, a prickly tropical plant sometimes grown outside in summer. Jotham's bramble (Judges 9:14–15), however, may have been the boxwood *(Lycium europaeum)*; other less prickly species of *Lycium* are to be seen in one of these beds.

Urticaceae The nettle family. Nettles of various species, including the Roman nettle *(Urtica pilulifera)*, are to be seen in this bed. In the scriptures they are referred to in connection with desolate places (Isaiah 34:13, Hosea 9:6).

Umbelliferae This family contains the parsley and parsnip.

Cummin or cumin *(Cuminum cyminum)* was mentioned by the prophet Isaiah as a plant that was carefully threshed with a rod and not crushed by a wheel (Isaiah 28:25–27 AV anise). This white-flowered herb is related to the yellow-flowered dill *(Anethum graveolens)*. Dill was one of the spices, together with cummin, rue and mint, that was carefully tithed by the Scribes and Pharisees who neglected justice and the love of God (Matthew 23:23, Luke 11:42).

Also present in the *Umbelliferae* beds are species of the giant fennel *(Ferula)* that are similar to *F. galbaniflua*, which yielded galbanum resin used by Jewish priests in the Holy Incense

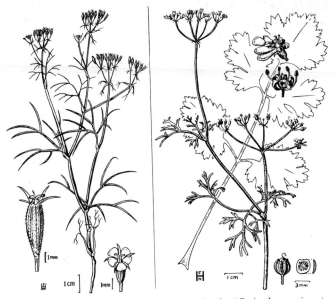

LEFT: cummin *(cuminum cyminum)*. RIGHT: coriander *(Coriandrum sativum)* with flowers, fruit and basal leaf

(Exodus 30:34). The resin is displayed in Museum No. 1. Also in this Museum are ancient Egyptian examples of the seeds of dill, already mentioned, and coriander *(Coriandrum sativum)*. The latter was familiar to the Israelites in Egypt, and during their wanderings in the Sinai Desert they said that manna reminded them of the appearance of coriander seeds (Exodus 16:31, Numbers 11:7).

The hemlock *(Conium maculatum)* that poisoned Socrates may have been the plant referred to in the Authorised Version of the Bible by that name (Hosea 10:4); other versions mention 'poisonous weeds' of arable land.

Valerianaceae   For nard, spikenard *(Nardostachys jatamansi)* see p. 42.

3 Corn, wine and oil
Cereals, grape-vine and olive tree

There were plentiful supplies of flour, . . . raisin cakes,
wine, oil . . . for there was joy in Israel.
(1 Chronicles 12:40 NIV)

ereals were only marginally more important than the other two core crops of the ancient Holy Land. The best flour was made from 'bread wheat' *(Triticum aestivum)* or in Old Testament times from 'emmer wheat' *(T. dicoccum)* or the hard 'macaroni wheat' *(T. durum)*. Wheat requires better soil and a longer time to grow than barley *(Hordeum vulgare)*, which was the staple food of the peasants. After harvest, fallen ears were often gleaned by the poor and foreigners, such as Ruth (Leviticus 23:22; Ruth 2:17).

Biblical references to corn or grain, bread, chaff and straw are numerous. For example, straw was used by the captive Israelites to make mud bricks in Egypt (Exodus 5:7). Jesus described Himself as the bread of life (John 6:35) and His body as broken bread (Matthew 26:26). The wild ancestors of these grains occur in the Bible lands where agriculture also began.

At Kew a large demonstration of cultivated cereals and their wild relatives can be seen in the grass collection near Greenhouse No.5 and there is an exhibit on cereals in Museum No.1. In one of the beds is planted the darnel grass *(Lolium temulentum)* referred to in Jesus' 'parable of the tares', which were the weeds growing among the wheat (Matthew 13:24–30). Its leaves are almost indistinguishable from those of the wheat and it is only positively recognized when its own ears develop – and they contain poisonous grains that adulterate the flour if harvested.

The grape vine *(Vitis vinifera)* has long trailing branches with tendrils and lobed leaves, as can be seen appropriately on the

Ears of **a** emmer wheat *(Triticum dicoccum)* **b** macaroni wheat *(T. durum)*
c, d two modern bread wheats **e** barley *(Hordeum vulgare)* all after
Schiemann. **f** Plant of darnel or tare *(Lolium temulentum)*

pergola of the Restaurant. A purple-leaved variety is grown against walls at Kew in the Cambridge Cottage Garden and in the Queen's Garden. In biblical times, as today, the Holy Land supported numerous vineyards and the grapes were eaten fresh or dried as raisins (Psalm 107:37; 1 Samuel 25:18). But they were primarily used for wine, which was produced from the grape juice pressed out of the fruit and fermented. The people of Israel were symbolized by the vine (Psalm 80:8–16; Isaiah 5:1–7). Jesus used the vine and vineyard in several of His illustrations (Matthew 21:33–46), even calling Himself the true vine (John 15:1) and likening wine to His blood at the Lord's Supper (Matthew 26:28).

Just as symbolic as the vine is the olive tree *(Olea europaea)*. The oil so frequently mentioned in the Bible was olive oil produced from its fruit. The oil was used for food (1 Kings 17:12), in lamps (Matthew 25:3), as medicine (Luke 10:34), in ritual offerings (Leviticus 2:4) and anointing kings (1 Samuel 10:1), being symbolic of the Holy Spirit. Olive trees provide a characteristic haze over the Mediterranean landscape, where they are planted in extensive groves on the terraced hillsides. Ancient trees often sprout new shoots from the base of their huge knobbly old trunks, as the psalmist knew (Psalm 128:3). Young trees have been planted in the Temperate House, where there is also the wild olive *(O. europaea* var. *sylvestris)* used for booths (Nehemiah 8:15) and mentioned by Paul (Romans 11:17). A shrubby small-leaved form of the olive, which may also be the wild one, does not flower or fruit even though it is protected by the wall of the Cambridge Cottage Garden. As a point of interest, a large tree growing outside in the Chelsea Physic Garden, London, flowers well each year and in 1976 fifteen pounds of fruit were collected from it. A cutting from that tree has been planted in the Queen's Garden at Kew and it is hoped that it will do as well. In Museum No. 1 olive oil can be seen, while in the Marianne North Gallery there is a painting of a fruiting olive branch and an example of its timber.

4 Pomegranates and almonds
Fruits and nuts wherever they occur

*A land of wheat and barley, of vines and fig trees and
pomegranates, a land of olive trees and honey.*
(Deuteronomy 8:8 RSV)

ruit orchards were important in biblical times, as is
shown by their frequent mention in the Scriptures,
where they are called gardens. In the last chapter we
looked at four of the famous seven fruits of the land listed in the
above quotation. Two of them were cereals and, apart from the
olive and the vine, the common fig *(Ficus carica)* was the most
valuable fruit. A fig tree grown beside the house (like the one in
the Queen's Garden) gave shade, as well as fruit, and under it
one could sit in peace (Micah 4:4). Large, lobed leaves clothed
Adam and Eve (Genesis 3:7), and Jesus used the figtree in
several of his illustrations (Luke 13:6–9, 21:29–31) and one was
cursed by Him (Mark 11:13, 20).

It is worth mentioning that the sycomore of the Bible is
another fig *(Ficus sycomorus)* – a small example grows in the
Palm House. It requires a warm, dry climate, such as that at
Jericho where the small man Zacchaeus climbed one to see
Jesus pass by (Luke 19:4). This large tree was as useful for its
timber as it was for its fruit (Amos 7:14). Wooden objects
made of sycomore are on display in Museum No.1. It should
not be confused with what we call the sycamore, which is a
European tree, *Acer pseudoplatanus*, while in America the name
sycamore applies to the plane-tree *(Platanus)*. Neither is it the
sycamine of the New Testament which Jesus referred to in
connection with believing faith (Luke 17:6 AV, RSV sycamine;
NEB, TEV, NIV mulberry). This is the black mulberry *(Morus
nigra)* that has rough leaves and blood-red fruits looking like

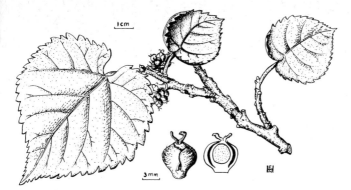

Black mulberry *(Morus nigra)* with female flowers

raspberries. There is a small tree of it in the sunken part of the
Queen's Garden, and another to the west of the Broad Walk.
The white mulberry *(M. alba)*, the food of silkworms, comes
from China and was not introduced into the Mediterranean until
the Middle Ages.

Beside the fig tree in the Queen's Garden is an apricot
(Prunus armenaica). Its white flowers appear in early spring but
the fruits usually do not develop in our climate. Apricots are
widely grown in the Mediterranean orchards where they enjoy
the hot dry summers. Some authors believe they were the apples
of gold in Proverbs 25:11.

Closely related to the apricot is the well-known almond
(Prunus dulcis). Leafless almond trees can be seen at Kew and
in private gardens flowering in early spring. Its Hebrew name
means 'waker' as its flowering precedes most other plants, hence
the play on words in Jeremiah 1:11. However, Aaron's almond
rod flowered and fruited overnight! (Numbers 17:1–10).
Almond flowers gave inspiration for the design of the Israelites'
lampstand (Exodus 25:33–36, 37:19–20). Some fragrant almond
nuts were taken to Egypt by Joseph's brothers (Genesis 43:11).

Another well-known nut is the walnut *(Juglans regia)*,
several large trees of which grow at Kew. This is said to be the

tree that bore the nuts referred to in Song of Solomon 6:11. It is not always easy to be sure to which plant a fruit or nut belongs. Some writers believe that the fruit of the green pine tree of Hosea 14:8 were the edible seeds of the stone pine *(Pinus pinea)*, a common Mediterranean tree, a fine specimen of which occurs near the Cambridge Cottage Garden and another grows near the western end of the Lake. The nuts taken to Joseph in Egypt were from *Pistacia terebinthus* and *P. atlantica*, not the pistachio, *P. vera* (see p. 14).

In Old Testament times the characteristic shape of the pomegranate fruit was used to decorate pillars of Solomon's Temple (1 Kings 7:20), as well as the hem of the high priest's robes (Exodus 28:33). The pomegranate *(Punica granatum)* is a bush with deep-green leaves and scarlet flowers in summer. There is a fine painting of a flowering bush in the Marianne North Gallery. A dwarf variety *(nana)* is grown in the Queen's Garden and in the border on the south side of Cambridge Cottage Garden wall, while full-sized double and yellow-flowered forms may be seen at the far end of Cambridge Cottage Garden. Typical red-flowered pomegranates grow in the Temperate House, where the carob tree also enjoys protection from winter frost. The carob *(Ceratonia siliqua)* is a small leguminous tree best known for its husks or pods that the Prodigal Son fed to the pigs and he himself ate in the time of famine (Luke 15:16). John the Baptist is also said to have eaten them (Matthew 3:4), hence their other common names, St John's bread and locust bean, although he may actually have eaten locust insects. The pods develop from the petal-less flowers on the branches in the autumn. Carob seeds are sufficiently constant in weight for the ancient Greeks to have used them as a measure for gold, hence our usage of the word 'carat'.

Readers may wonder why 'honey' is counted as a fruit. Although some biblical references to honey indicate that made by bees from nectar, Deuteronomy 8:8 refers to the syrup obtained from dates (see p. 49).

A walnut tree *(Juglans regia)* planted in 1959 by Queen Elizabeth II in front of Kew Palace (p. 31)

The stone pine *(Pinus pinea)* produces edible seeds (p. 32)

Bitter aloes *(Aloe barbadense)* were used at Jesus's burial (p. 37)

◁ Flowers of the pomegranate *(Punica granatum)* painted by Marianne North
(p. 32)

Ladanum resin of the Bible was obtained from the white rock rose *Cistus laurifolius* of Asia – a hybrid of it, *C.* × *cyprius*, shown here, flowers at Kew (p. 38). The pink *Cistus creticus* occurs on hillsides in the Holy Land (p. 38)

5 Frankincense and myrrh
Fragrant and medicinal plants

Dead flies give perfume a bad smell. (Ecclesiastes 10:1 NIV)

ragrant and resinous plants were in demand in biblical times for cosmetics and medicines, but they are not always easy to identify from their Hebrew names. Caravans of camels bearing spices travelled the Incense Routes of Arabia to the centres of civilization, where only the rich could afford the costly produce.

The most famous incense came from north-east Africa and southern Arabia where frankincense *(Boswellia carteri, B. papyrifera, B. sacra)*, myrrh *(Commiphora molmol, C. myrrha)* and balm-of-Gilead *(Commiphora gileadensis)* were tapped. These trees and shrubs yield resins from incisions made in their branches. Frankincense was burnt together with other spices (Exodus 30:1), while ground myrrh was used for other religious ceremonies, medicines and perfumery (Exodus 30:23, Song of Solomon 3:6). Gifts of gold, frankincense and myrrh were brought by the three wise men to the infant Jesus (Matthew 2:11) and myrrh was used at his burial (John 19:39). Sometimes examples of *Boswellia* and *Commiphora* are exhibited in Greenhouse No. 5 but they are not necessarily of the very species yielding the resin; however, samples of the resin are on display in Museum No. 1 by the Pond.

Also in Greenhouse No. 5 is a large plant of aloe *(Aloe barbadense)*. It has stiff fleshy leaves with sharp marginal teeth and very bitter juice. The yellowish flowers appear early in spring. The powdered leaves were mixed with myrrh for embalming and it was Nicodemus who took 30 kg or 100 pounds weight of the costly mixture to the garden tomb after the crucifixion of Jesus (John 19:39). This aloe can also be seen in Museum No. 1 and in the Marianne North Gallery. The 'aloes' of the Old Testament (Psalm 45:8, Proverbs 7:17) are, however, entirely different, being a rare tree native to Assam and Burma and known as the lign-aloe or eaglewood *(Aquilaria agallocha)*, which is not grown at Kew.

A few of the resinous plants used for balm in biblical times grow happily outside at Kew. Various species yield gummy resin that was applied to wounds as a balm or ointment and we cannot be sure which ones were involved. When the Midianite traders took Joseph as a slave into Egypt they also carried 'gum, balm and myrrh' (Genesis 37:25). The 'gum' was probably the gum tragacanth obtained from *Astragalus gummifer*, a spiny cushion vetch of rocky hillsides in Iran – a dried specimen and lump of the resin are on view in Museum No. 1, while non-spiny species of this large genus can be seen in the Herbaceous Ground and in the Rock Garden. A likely source of 'balm' was the low lentisk bush *(Pistacia lentiscus)*, which is common in the Mediterranean region and yields mastic resin. A plant of it grows in the southern portion of the Temperate House and its resin is on display in Museum No. 1. The third substance, 'myrrh', is unlikely to have been the tropical product of that name, but 'ladanum' from rock roses *(Cistus laurifolius)*. At Kew *C. creticus* and *C.* × *cyprius*, which is a hybrid between Spanish *C. ladanifer* and the Turkish *C. laurifolius*, grow beside King William's Temple, where they flower profusely in June and July. Ancient writers record that this ladanum resin, which is produced by the leaves of these shrubs, was collected by herdsmen who combed the beards of the goats that had browsed among them all day!

The substance called 'stacte' used in the Sacred Incense of Jewish rites (Exodus 30:34) is reputed to have been a resin obtained from the storax tree, *Styrax officinalis*. A bush of this has been planted in a corner of Cambridge Cottage Garden where it produces a mass of white bell-like flowers in June. Another possible source of the stacte was the resin from the Levant storax or oriental sweet gum, *Liquidambar orientalis*. A rounded tree with graceful weeping branches grows near the Magnolia Dell (beside it is the taller American sweet gum, *L. styraciflua*). However, storax may well have been balm of Gilead *(Commiphora gileadensis)*, mentioned above.

If you take a walk to the Queen's Garden behind Kew Palace you will find a fascinating bower laid out in seventeenth-century style with many old-fashioned plants. Some of them were introduced during the early Christian period from the Mediterranean region where they were known by the Romans in New Testament times. They are the kind of plants that continued to be grown in old monastery gardens during the Middle Ages and many of them are fragrant and have medicinal value.

Near the gazebo is a cluster of plants from the Holy Land including the myrtle *(Myrtus communis)*, and Madonna lily *(Lilium candidum)*. The latter, though not actually mentioned in the Bible (except possibly as one of the lilies) was often featured in religious paintings of the Middle Ages. The myrtle, however, was one of the desirable plants Isaiah expected to replace the desert thorn (or brier) in that promised day of the Lord (Isaiah 41:19, 55:13). For many centuries Jews have used its evergreen branches for the construction of booths at the Feast of Tabernacles (Nehemiah 8:15). At Kew only in the severest winters are the leaves frosted and in summer this fragrant bush is covered with sweet smelling white flowers.

Other plants near the gazebo include the milk thistle *(Silybum marianum)*, Jerusalem sage *(Phlomis viscosa)*, red topped sage *(Salvia horminum)*, goat St John's Wort *(Hypericum hircinum)* and the Judas tree *(Cercis siliquastrum)*. The non-biblical tradition is that Judas hung himself from this tree (Matthew 27:5), hence its white flowers turned red like blood issuing from its branches. A similar story goes with the passion flower *(Passiflora caerulea)*, which was so named by the Roman

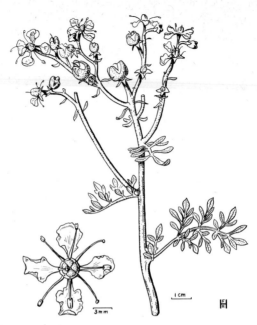

Rue *(Ruta graveolens)*

Catholic missionaries in South America who likened the curious arrangement of the styles to the implements used at the crucifixion of Christ. There are many such traditional, non-biblical plants which are not dealt with in this booklet.

Nearby in the sunken part of this Garden common and unusual pot herbs tumble over one another in a profusion of growth; there are many fragrant plants. A very rankly scented species is the rue *(Ruta graveolens)*, which has grey-green leaves throughout the year and yellow flowers in summer. The more straggly wild rue of the Holy Land *(R. chalepensis)*, one of the herbs tithed by the Scribes and Pharisees (see p. 25), can be seen in the Cambridge Cottage Garden.

One could be misled into thinking that the 'hyssop' *(Hyssopus*

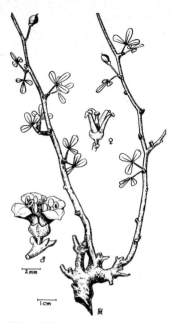

Balm of Gilead *(Commiphora gileadensis)*   Saffron crocus *(Crocus sativus)*

officinale) growing here would be the biblical plant. In fact *Hyssopus* is a southern European species that is unlikely to have been known in the Holy Land. There is a further difficulty in that three distinct plants are referred to in the Bible as 'hyssop'. The one used in the Jewish sacrificial rites (Exodus 12:22) is thought to have been a white marjoram *(Majorana syriaca* also called *Origanum syriacum* and *O. maru)*, which is a fragrant wiry plant related to sweet marjoram *(O. majorana)*, also growing in the sunken area. The second 'hyssop' that grew out of walls (1 Kings 4:33) was probably the prickly caper bush *(Capparis spinosa)*, too tender for cultivation outside at Kew but it is grown in the Temperate House. It is also called 'desire' in Ecclesiastes 12:5 (AV, RSV). A third 'hyssop' appears in some

41

versions of the Bible as the object on which a sponge was supported while Jesus was on the cross (John 19:29). It was probably a rod or reed, but there is a tradition that it was a stalk of dura *(Sorghum bicolor)*, a tall cereal which sometimes can be seen during the summer in the Grass Garden.

The 'sweet cane' or 'calamus' of Exodus 30:23 and Song of Solomon 4:14 is not a grass or reed, but the sweet flag *Acorus calamus*, a member of the arum family, that grows in the mud around the Lake at Kew. Its dried rhizomes used to be imported into Jerusalem from Central Asia for the sake of their fragrant properties. Another plant mentioned in Song of Solomon 4:14 is the spikenard (RSV nard) which was distilled from the desert camel grass *(Cymbopogon schoenanthus)*, related to the tropical citronella oil grass *(C. nardus)* shown in Museum No. 1. But the precious perfume that Mary used to anoint Jesus's feet (John 12:3) is thought to have been purified from the stem of the perennial Himalayan valerian *(Nardostachys jatamansi)*.

Associated with these perfumes in Song of Solomon 4:14 is saffron – a yellow substance obtained from the stigmas of the saffron crocus *(Crocus sativus)*. This mauve, autumn-flowering species does not take kindly to the moist English climate, so it rarely flowers in the Queen's Garden, but it is similar to the garden crocuses that provide a splendid show at Kew in early spring. In Song of Solomon 2:1 and Isaiah 35:1 the Hebrew word for 'crocus' is often translated into English as 'rose'. Writers on biblical plants agree that 'rose' is not *Rosa* and that *Crocus* species, the white narcissus *(N. tazetta)* or scarlet tulip *(Tulipa montana, T. sharonensis)* are more likely. The NEB uses the word 'asphodel' instead of crocus or rose in Isaiah 35:1 (see p. 20). This could be either the white asphodel *(Asphodelus microcarpus)* or the yellow asphodel *(Asphodeline lutea)*, both of them occurring in the Holy Land. Many species of bulbs and corms are grown throughout Kew, especially in the Cambridge Cottage Garden and the Queen's Garden.

6 Reeds, waterlilies and gourds
Water plants and some tropical plants

Can papyrus grow where there is no marsh? Can reeds
flourish where there is no water? (Job 8:11 RSV)

n the Aquatic Garden there is a reed-mace or cat-tail
(Typha latifolia), similar to the Egyptian *T. domingensis*
among which baby Moses' papyrus basket was floating
(Exodus 2:3–5 AV, RSV bulrush). Nearby is the flowering rush
(Butomus umbellatus) with pink flowers in summer which some
writers consider to be the 'reeds' of Job 8:11 quoted at the head
of this chapter. In the boggy parts of the Aquatic Garden various
rushes *(Juncus* species) can be seen – rushes are mentioned or
implied in several scriptures (e.g. Genesis 41:2). The sweet flag
(Acorus calamus) is also there (see p. 42) and some waterlilies
(Nymphaea), discussed below.

The common reed *(Phragmites australis,* formerly *P.
communis)*, which was used to make arrows (1 Samuel 20:20)
and pens (3 John:13), grows in the Grass Garden pool. The
giant reed *(Arundo donax)*, which also occurs in the Holy Land,
is tender. It is sometimes grown at Kew in the Grass Garden,
where it tolerates drier conditions than the common reed.

The large pool in the middle of the hot and steamy Greenhouse No.15 is decorated with the floating leaves and the
colourful flowers of waterlilies *(Nymphaea)*. In ancient times
the waterlilies flourishing in the backwaters of the River Nile
were known by the Egyptians as 'lotus'. Since Herodotus' time
(484–424 BC) there has been confusion as to the identity of the
ancient Egyptian aquatic lotus. The Far Eastern sacred lotus,
Nelumbo nucifera, which he described, must have been introduced into Egypt shortly before his time as it is not depicted in

43

dynastic wall-paintings nor are the seeds found in early excavations. *Nelumbo* plants may be seen in House No.15 and its seeds are shown in the Museum.

The white flowered *Nymphaea lotus* and the fragrant blue *N. caerulea* were often featured in ornamental and symbolic works of art, such as in the painting displayed in No.1 Museum, where there is also an ancient Egyptian garland containing lotus petals. So, it is hardly surprising that the Israelites should also have adopted the design of 'lily work' to ornament the pillars in King Solomon's Temple (1 Kings 7:19).

At one side of the same pool there is a large clump of the paper sedge *(Cyperus papyrus)* which has distinctive mop-like flower heads. One of Marianne North's pictures shows a papyrus swamp in Sicily. Quite recently Thor Heyerdahl used the buoyant stalk for the construction of his trans-Atlantic Ra I and Ra II, like the ancient Egyptians' papyrus boats of various sizes (Isaiah 18:2). Its most famous use, however, was for the manufacture of the papyrus writing material from its pith. The Greeks called the white pith inside the three angled stalks *byblos* and the books composed of papyrus sheets *bybla* – from which our word 'Bible' is derived. To make papyrus in the ancient manner strips of the pith are placed side by side with another layer on top at right angles, and the whole pressed together and dried to form a sheet. Scribes wrote with rush or reed pens and ink of carbon scraped from cooking vessels.

Above your head you will notice the various gourds climbing. They may include the water-melon *(Citrullus lanatus)* and the musk-melon *(Cucumis melo)*, which were the melons and cucumbers the Israelites longed for in the desert during their exodus from Egypt (Numbers 11:5). Another gourd, though not one grown at Kew since it needs hot dry places, is the colocynth *(Citrullus colocynthis)* that almost poisoned Elisha's young men when they collected the attractive yellow fruits for the pot (2 Kings 4:39). Some of these fruits are on display in the Museum No.1.

A bush of storax *(Styrax officinalis)* in full flower in the Cambridge Cottage Garden (p. 38)

Both the flowers and leaves of myrtle *(Myrtus communis)* are fragrant (p. 39)

OPPOSITE: Tall papyrus *(Cyperus papyrus)* and a white waterlily *(Nymphaea lotus)* in tropical Greenhouse No. 15 (p. 44) ▷

A date palm *(Phoenix dactylifera)* painted by Marianne North (p. 49)

7 Palms and other tropical plants
Those in the Palm House

The righteous shall flourish like the palm tree.
(Psalm 92:12 AV)

everal tropical and sub-tropical plants, other than those mentioned in Chapter 6, are grown in the Palm House. There is even a date palm *(Phoenix dactylifera)* – a small one since a full-grown one would burst through the roof! The palm tree's tall straight trunk was a symbol of elegance to the Hebrews who named girls Tamar after it (2 Samuel 13:1). Its huge feathery leaves (called branches in John 12:13) were cut by the crowd welcoming Jesus during his triumphant entry into Jerusalem: palm leaves have long been a symbol of victory. Dates were used to make syrup, called 'honey' in Deuteronomy 8:8. Some old date stones can be seen in Museum No.1, and paintings of the trees in the Marianne North Gallery.

The tropical shrub henna *(Lawsonia inermis)* has numerous small white flowers with a very sweet fragrance that Solomon knew (Song of Solomon 1:14, 4:13). Its crushed leaves provided a yellow dye for staining skin and nails of ancient Egyptian mummies and it is still popular for colouring human hair and horses' tails. A shrub of it grows in the Palm House, while dried samples are in Museum No.1.

The cinnamon *(Cinnamomum zeylanicum)* bush also growing in the Palm House is easily recognized by its prominently 3-nerved leaves. Similar to it, but not grown at Kew, is the cassia bush *(Cinnamomum cassia)*. They both yield fragrant barks, which according to tradition, were the cinnamon and cassia of the Old Testament (Exodus 30:23–24). They must have been very rare and expensive in those days since the trees

49

grow in Sri Lanka and the Far East respectively. Samples of cinnamon bark are shown in Museum No.1, and there is a painting of a flowering shoot in the Marianne North Gallery.

Examples of acacia are also present in the Palm House, but not of the species *(Acacia tortilis* subspecies *raddiana* and *A. albida)* that would have been used to make the Tabernacle, or tent of meeting, constructed by the Israelites in Sinai (Exodus 37:25). These thorny trees were called *shittim* in Hebrew, hence the use of this word in the AV. Acacias are almost the only timber trees available in that desert.

Algum, one of the tropical hardwoods imported by Solomon (1 Kings 10:11), may have been either red sandalwood *(Pterocarpus santalum)* or white sandalwood *(Santalum album)*. Both are Indian trees and examples of their timber are in the Wood Museum. Ebony was mentioned by the prophet Ezekiel (27:15). In ancient Egypt the almost black timber called ebony used for fine furniture came from a leguminous tree *Dalbergia melanoxylon* from tropical Africa, but later the name was transferred to a truly black timber obtained from the tropical Asian *Diospyros ebenum*, that we now know as ebony. There are examples of both these trees in the Palm House and carved ebony elephants in the Wood Museum.

The curtains in the King's palace at Susa were made of cotton (Esther 1:6), which was unusual and expensive in those days. Cotton plants *(Gossypium herbaceum)* are grown each year in the Palm House, where the white bolls mature in late summer. The yellow flowers appear in one of Marianne North's pictures.

God gave Solomon wisdom and understanding . . . He spoke of trees from the cedar that is in Lebanon to the hyssop that grows out of the wall; he spoke also of beasts, and of birds and of reptiles, and of fish. And men came from all peoples to hear the wisdom of Solomon . . . . (1 Kings 4:29 . . . 34 RSV)

Further reading

Popular illustrated works

Anderson, D. A. (1979) *All the trees and woody plants of the Bible* Texas, Word Books.

Cole, Sonia (1970) *The Neolithic Revolution* London, British Museum, Natural History, 72 pages. An account of the beginnings of agriculture in the Bible lands and Europe. Out of print.

Goor, A. & Nurock, M. (1968) *The Fruits of the Holy Land* Jerusalem, Israel Universities Press, 293 pages. Includes notes from the Talmud and Mishnah, as well as the Bible, and more recent observations.

Hareuveni, Nogah (1974) *Ecology in the Bible* Israel, Neot Kedumim, Kiryat Ono, 52 pages. An illustrated booklet.

Hareuveni, Nogah (1980) *Nature in our Biblical Heritage* Israel, Neot Kedumin.

Hillier, N., Johnson, J.D. & Wiseman, D.J. (eds.) (1980) *The Illustrated Bible Dictionary* Leicester, Inter-Varsity Press, 3 vols. Botanical entries by F. Nigel Hepper.

Polunin, Oleg & Huxley, Anthony (1978) *Flowers of the Mediterranean* London, Chatto & Windus, 257 pages. Useful for identification, including some species to be seen in the Eastern Mediterranean, with notes on ancient and biblical plants.

Vedel, H. (1978) *Trees and Shrubs of the Mediterranean* Harmondsworth, Penguin Nature Guides, 127 pages. Includes native and exotic species for the traveller, with notes on trees in religion.

Text-books and older standard references

Donkin, R. A. (1980) *Manna: an historical geography* The Hague, Junk.

Löw, Immanuel (1926–34) *Die flora der Juden* Vienna, Kohut-Foundation, 4 vols. Reprinted 1967. An exhaustive treatment of plants associated with the Jews; in German.

Moldenke, H.N. & A.L. (1952) *Plants of the Bible* New York, Ronald Press Co. 328 pages.

Mouterde, P. (1966–79) *Nouvelle flore du Liban et de la Syrie* Beirut, 3 vols. In French; illustrated by line drawings.

Post, G.E. & Dinsmore, J.E. (1933) *Flora of Syria, Palestine and Sinai* Beirut, second edition, 2 vols.

Smith, John (1878) *History of Bible Plants* London. The author was Curator of the living collections at Kew 1841–64; the 10 lithographic plates were drawn by W.H.Fitch, who was the official artist at Kew.

Smith, William (ed.) (1863) *Dictionary of the Bible* London. Second edition, 3 vols (1893). The botanical entries were written by Sir Joseph Hooker who was Assistant Director of Kew 1855–65 and Director 1865–85.

Täckholm, V. & Drar, M. (1941–) *Flora of Egypt* Cairo, 4 vols. In English; a projected multi-volume work, including extensive notes on the plants in ancient Egypt.

Täckholm, Vivi (1974) *Students' Flora of Egypt* Cairo, second edition, 888 pages. With concise keys and descriptions'

Townsend, C.C. & Guest, E. (1966–) *Flora of Iraq* Baghdad, multi-volume work prepared at Kew; descriptions of plants with notes on their uses.

Tristram, H.B. (1867) *The Natural History of the Bible* London, second edition, 518 pages (1868).

Zohary, Michael (1962) *Plant-life of Palestine* New York, Ronald Press Co. 262 pages. An erudite descriptive account of the vegetation of the Holy Land.

Zohary, Michael & Feinbrun, Naomi (1966–) *Flora Palaestina* Jerusalem: Israel Academy of Sciences, 4 vols text and 4 vols figures. In English; three of the four volumes have been issued, most of the species are illustrated by line drawing. It covers present day Israel and parts of Jordan on both sides of the R. Jordan.

An Ancient Egyptian garden showing date palms and trees around a pool with lotus water lilies

Index I
References in the Bible

NOTE: the references provided in the text are very selective but they provide at least one reference to each plant or plant product mentioned.

Old Testament

Index II
English plant names

Page references in *italics* are to illustrations

Index III
Scientific plant names and locations

The authors of the plant names are provided, usually in an abbreviated form. The plant family to which each species belongs is enclosed in round brackets ( ). Non-biblical species mentioned incidentally are in square brackets [ ]. Some synonyms are provided. Common names appear in the text.

 Grid references (e.g. J16) are to selected localities of those species represented at Kew (see map on page 2), text page numbers are in **bold** and illustration page numbers in *italics*. MNG=Marianne North Gallery.

Lens esculenta Moench see *L. culinaris*
Lilium candidum L. (Liliaceae)   **19, 39**   D16 Queen's Garden
Linum usitatissimum L. (Linaceae)   *12,* **20**   J13 Museum No. 1,
   J15 Herbaceous Ground, L7 MNG design on door frame
Liquidambar orientalis Mill. (Hamamelidaceae)   **39**   E10
[*Liquidambar styraciflua* L. (Hamamelidaceae)   **39**   E10]
Lolium temulentum L. (Gramineae)   **27,** *28*   H15 Grass Garden
Lycium europaeum L. (Solanaceae)   **25**   J15 Herbaceous Ground
[*Lycium* species (Solanaceae)   **25**   J15 Herbaceous Ground]
Majorana syriaca (L.) Rafin. (Labiatae)   **41**
Mandragora officinarum L. (Solanaceae)   **25**   D16 Queen's Garden,
   J13 Museum No. 1
Mentha longifolia (L.) Huds. (Labiatae)   **19**   J15 Herbaceous Ground
[*Morus alba* L. (Moraceae)   **31**   H10]
Morus nigra L. (Moraceae)   **30,** *31*   D16 Queen's Garden, G14
Myrtus communis L. (Myrtaceae)   **39,** *46*   D16 Queen's Garden, H17
   Cambridge Cottage Garden, J6 Temperate House, J13 Museum No. 1
Narcissus species (Amaryllidaceae)   **42**   H17 Cambridge Cottage Garden
Narcissus tazetta L. (Amaryllidaceae)   **42**   J13 Museum No. 1, J15
   Herbaceous Ground
Nardostachys jatamansi (D. Don) DC. (Valerianaceae)   **42**
[*Nelumbo nucifera* Gaertn.   **43**   G13 Greenhouse No. 15, J13 Museum No. 1,
   L7 MNG pictures 294, 684]
Nerium oleander L. (Apocynaceae)   *11,* **16**   D16 Queen's Garden,
   J6 Temperate House, L7 MNG pictures 125, 341
Nigella sativa L. (Ranunculaceae)   **20**   J15 Herbaceous Ground
Notobasis syriaca (L.) Cass. (Compositae)   **17**   J15 Herbaceous Ground
Nymphaea species (Nymphaeaceae)   **43**   G13 Greenhouse No. 15,
   J16 Aquatic Garden, L7 MNG pictures 455, 818
Nymphaea caerulea Sav. (Nymphaeaceae)   **44**   J13 Museum No. 1
Nymphaea lotus L. (Nymphaeaceae)   **44,** *47*   G13 Greenhouse No. 15
Olea europaea L. (Oleaceae)   **29**   D16 Queen's Garden, J6 Temperate
   House, J13 Museum No. 1, J17 Wall border, L7 MNG picture 517,
   timber 156
Olea europaea L. var. *sylvestris* (Mill.) Brot. (Oleaceae)   **29**   J6 Temperate
   House
Origanum maru L. (Labiatae) see *Majorana syriaca*
Origanum syriacum L. (Labiatae) see *Majorana syriaca*
[*Origanum majorana* L. (Labiatae)   **41**   D16 Queen's Garden]
Ornithogalum narbonense L. (Liliaceae)   **19,** *22*   H17 Cambridge Cottage
   Garden, J15 Herbaceous Ground, L7 MNG picture 394
Paliurus spina-christi Mill. (Celastraceae)   **14,** *15*   L6

Papaver species (Papaveraceae) *Cover*, **20** J15 Herbaceous Ground

[*Passiflora caerulea* L. (Passifloraceae) **39** cf L7 MNG picture 112]

[*Phlomis viscosa* Poir. (Labiatae) **39** D16 Queen's Garden]

Phoenix dactylifera L. (Palmae) *48, 49* H12 Palm House, J13 Museum
No. 1, L7 MNG pictures 366, 514

Phragmites australis (Cav.) Steud. (Gramineae) **43**, *47* H15 Grass
Garden pool

Phragmites communis Trin. see *P. australis*

Pinus halepensis Mill. (Pinaceae) **8**, *9* D5, F13, G15, J13 Wood Museum

Pinus pinea L. (Pinaceae) **32**, *33* D5, H16

Pistacia atlantica Desf. (Anacardiaceae) **13, 14** J6 Temperate House

Pistacia lentiscus L. (Anacardiaceae) **14, 38** J6 Temperate House,
J13 Museum No. 1

Pistacia palaestina (Boiss.) Kotschy (Anacardiaceae) **14**

Pistacia terebinthus L. (Anacardiaceae) **14** J6 Temperate House, L16

[*Pistacia vera* L. **32**]

Platanus orientalis L. (Platanaceae) *10*, **15, 16** E15, F16

Populus alba L. (Salicaceae) **15** B2, K4

Populus euphratica Oliv. (Salicaceae) **15**

Poterium spinosum L. (Rosaceae) **14** J15 Rock Garden

Prunus amygdalus Batsch see *P. dulcis*

Prunus armeniaca L. (Rosaceae) *24*, **31** D16 Queen's Garden

Prunus dulcis (Mill.) D.A. Webb (Rosaceae) *24*, **31** E13, F4, J12, J13
Museum No. 1, K13, 14

Pterocarpus santalinus L.f. (Leguminosae) **50** H17 Wood Museum

Punica granatum L. (Punicaceae) **32**, *34* H17 Cambridge Cottage Garden,
J6 Temperate House, J13 Museum No. 1, L7 MNG picture 502

Punica granatum L. var. *nana* (L.) Pers. **32** D16 Queen's Garden,
J17 Wall border

Quercus aegilops L. (Fagaceae) **13** C8. See also J13 Wood Museum

Quercus calliprinos Webb see *Q. coccifera* **13**

Quercus coccifera L. (Fagaceae) **13** C7

[*Quercus ilex* L. **13** D7 etc]

Quercus ithaburensis Decne. (Fagaceae) **13**, *13* C10

Retama raetam (Forssk.) Webb (Leguminosae) **16**

Ricinus communis L. (Euphorbiaceae) **18** J13 Museum No. 1, J15
Herbaceous Ground, L7 MNG picture 101

Ruta chalepensis L. (Rutaceae) **40** H17 Cambridge Cottage Garden,
J15 Herbaceous Ground

Ruta graveolens L. (Rutaceae) **40**, *40* D16 Queen's Garden, H17 Cambridge
Cottage Garden, J15 Herbaceous Ground

[*Salix babylonica* L. (Salicaceae) **15** E8, H13, L7 MNG picture 237]

Salix acmophylla Boiss. (Salicaceae)   **15**

Salix safsaf Forssk. see *S. subserrata*

Salix subserrata Willd.   **15**   J13 Museum No. 1

Salvia species (Labiatae)   **19**   D16 Queen's Garden, H17 Cambridge Cottage Garden, J15 Herbaceous Garden

[*Salvia horminum* L. (Labiatae)   **39**   D16 Queen's Garden, J15 Herbaceous Ground]

Salvia judaica Boiss. (Labiatae)   **19**

Santalum album L. (Santalaceae)   **50**   H17 Wood Museum, MNG picture 319, timber 74, 165

Sarcopoterium spinosum (L.) Sp. see *Poterium spinosum*

Scolymus maculatus L. (Compositae)   **18**, *21*   J15 Herbaceous Ground

Silybum marianum (L.) Gaertn. (Compositae)   **17**, *21*, **39**   D16 Queen's Garden, J15 Herbaceous Ground

Sinapis alba L. (Cruciferae)   **18**   J15 Herbaceous Ground

Sorghum bicolor (L.) Moench (Gramineae)   **42**   H15 Grass Garden

Sorghum vulgare Pers. see *S. bicolor*

Styrax officinalis L. (Styracaceae)   **38**, *45*   H17 Cambridge Cottage Garden

Tamarix gallica L. (Tamaricaceae)   **16**   K9

Tamarix gallica L. var. *mannifera* Ehrenb.   **16**

Tamarix parviflora DC. (Tamaricaceae)   **16**   E16, K9

Tamarix species (Tamaricaceae)   **16**   J13 Museum No. 1

Taraxacum officinale L. (Compositae)   **18**   J15 Herbaceous Ground

Tetraclinis articulata (Vahl) Mast. (Cupressaceae)   **14**   J6 Temperate House

Triticum aestivum L. (Gramineae)   **27**, *28*   H15 Grass Garden, J13 Museum No. 1

Triticum dicoccum Schrank (Gramineae)   **27**, *28*   H15 Grass Garden, J13 Museum No. 1

Triticum durum Desf. (Gramineae)   **27**, *28*   H15 Grass Garden, J13 Museum No. 1

Triticum vulgare Vill. see *T. aestivum*

Tulipa montana Lindl. (Liliaceae)   **42**   H17 Cambridge Cottage Garden

Tulipa sharonensis Dinsm. (Liliaceae)   **42**

Typha domingensis Pers. (Typhaceae)   **43**

[*Typha latifolia* L. (Typhaceae)   **43**   J16 Aquatic Garden]

Vicia faba L. (Leguminosae)   **19**   J15 Herbaceous Ground

Vitis vinifera L. (Vitidaceae)   *23*, **27**   D16 Queen's Garden, J13 Museum No. 1, J17 Cambridge Cottage Garden, K6 Refreshment Pavilion, L7 MNG picture 615

Ziziphus spina-christi (L.) Desf. (Rhamnaceae)   **14**, *15*   J6 Temperate House, J13 Museum No. 1

Printed in England for Her Majesty's Stationery Office by Staples Printers St Albans Limited at The Priory Press

Dd 696898 C40 — 10/80.